Martha the Pig

By William J. Vosper, Jr.

To order additional copies of this book, contact:
Xlibris
844-714-8691
www.Xlibris.com
Orders@Xlibris.com

William J. Vosper is an attorney in Stillwater, New
Jersey who runs Buckhill Farm in Hardwick, New
Jersey with his wife Sharon, the inspiration for Aunt
Kate. His stories about Buckhill Farm are based on the
real-life adventures of beloved farm animals. This book
was printed in the United States of America.

ISBN: 978-1-4134-3173-5 (sc)

Library of Congress Control Number: 2003096932

Print information available on the last page

Rev. date: 10/15/2020

CHAPTER 1

BABY MARTHA

Martha was the tiniest piglet ever born on Buckhill Farm. She was what every farmer called the runt of the litter. Aunt Kate, who lived on Buckhill Farm, found Martha to be no more than a handful when she picked her up. She was hardly bigger than a baby rabbit. Martha was so tiny that her brothers and sisters would always push her around. The other piglets never gave her a chance to nurse on their mother and they always pushed her away when they ate at the trough. All her brothers and sisters were growing; Martha was wasting away.

There were so many little piglets to feed that Aunt Kate needed to find more food. She made an arrangement with a local restaurant to take all their food scraps at the end of the day. Even with more food in the trough little Martha would still get pushed aside by all her growing brothers and sisters. Many nights Martha would not get anything to eat. She was so hungry and she was still so tiny.

Aunt Kate tried to take good care of every animal on Buckhill Farm. She loved them all and clucked over them like a mother hen. She knew Martha was a problem. She had noticed that tiny Martha was getting pushed around and was very hungry. Aunt Kate set aside the best tidbits from the scraps for Martha. Martha's favorite quickly became the leftover shrimps. Aunt Kate would pick all the shrimps from the scraps and give the remainder to the other piglets in their trough, but Martha would get a bowl of shrimps for herself. Eventually she was getting enough to eat and she began to grow.

CHAPTER 2

A TROUGH OF ONE'S OWN

All of Martha's big brothers and sisters were sold to other farms, but Martha still wasn't big enough to sell. She was the only pig left on Buckhill Farm. But now Martha didn't have anyone to push her away from her food; the trough was all hers. She would eat and eat and eat some more. She would sit down and eat and she would stand up and eat. She would even lie down and eat. She grew and grew and grew some more. Martha grew so big she weighed more than 600 pounds and she was still gaining weight.

At 600 pounds Martha was very big and very strong but she was very lonely now all her brothers and sisters were gone.

Martha's pigpen was set far from the farmhouse and she wished she could be nearer all her barnyard buddies. She wanted to play. She would put her feet up in the side of her pen and gaze wistfully towards the barnyard. One day something dramatic happened. With a crack and a crash her old wooden pigpen shattered and smashed. At last she was free and found herself outside looking in. Now Martha could play all day.

CHAPTER 3

FULL GROWN

Martha could now break out of her pen any time she wanted to walk around the farm. She would wander around until she found Farmer Butch and Farmer Bill. If they were up in the fields she would stroll up there and visit and if they were planting corn in another field she would find them. Once she had found them one would climb on her and she would give him a ride back to the barn oinking all the way.

Every morning at the crack of dawn Sam and Snookie, the geese, would start quacking and honking. They wanted everyone in the barnyard to get up and start the day. Martha loved being an early riser. It meant more time to eat.

At five in the morning she would stand under Aunt Kate's window oinking and snorting. Martha wanted her shrimp breakfast and she wanted it quickly. Aunt Kate must get up and Martha refused to be quiet and let her go back to sleep. Poor Aunt Kate would come down in her robe and slippers and give Martha her breakfast. Martha would then let Aunt Kate go back to bed. A happy pig is a full quiet pig.

But also a full pig is a growing pig. Aunt Kate had to buy extra shrimps for Martha. The more she gave her the more she ate. The more she ate the bigger she got and she was now 700 pounds. Martha was a big girl. In fact she was as big as Tony the Bull's daughter Harriet the Heifer.

CHAPTER 4

ADVENTURES

Martha was a headstrong and contrary pig and she knew her own mind. She knew just what she wanted to do and just where she wanted to go. She roamed all over Buckhill Farm playing with the other animals and looking for Aunt Kate or the farmers. After a while she would get bored.

About once a week she would go exploring. She would amble off down the road to the small town of Stillwater. She discovered all the wonders of other people's garbage cans.

Oh the glorious tastes from other kitchens; no garbage can was safe.

No store was safe either. If a shop left its doors open Martha would walk right in and look around. She tried, on many occasions, to get into the supermarket. Oh the smell made her mouth water. But she never seemed to get her head in those doors as they always closed before she could get in.

As pigs go Martha was a very social pig. She was happy to visit with anyone. She would stop and smell people's flowers, watch children playing or listen to people talking, usually about her. The police would try to stop her to go home but she would ignore them. She would only go home when she was tired of visiting and not before. When she was good and ready she would amble up the road back home.

After such a long walk and so many adventures Martha would need to find a cool and quiet place for a nap. The finest place was the stalls of Ben and Bows, the horses. She would settle down in the sweet-smelling hay and snore away the rest of the day.

Unfortunately pigs that eat from garbage cans tend to get quite smelly and smelly pigs attract horseflies. As pigs have very thick skins flies don't bother them so Martha didn't pay any attention to them. But poor Ben and Bows couldn't go near her. Horseflies love horses even better than pigs but sadly their skins weren't as tough as Martha's. This meant that Ben and Bows couldn't go into their stalls until Martha decided to go on her merry way taking the flies with her.

CHAPTER 5

PLAYTIME

After a great adventure and a nice nap Martha was ready to play again. She adored the other animals and would try to take turns playing with everyone. First she would visit the goats Brownie and Chocolate Chip who loved her. They would all run in circles until Martha stopped. Then one of the goats would jump on her back. She would give them rides around the barnyard.

Martha would then go and find the old German Shepard named Max. She knew he didn't like her but she loved to tease him. If she could catch him lying down out in the sun taking his nap, she would run at him like a run away steam engine, snorting and oinking trying to scare him. This worked beautifully. He would wake up, jump up and chase her all over the farm. But Martha wasn't scared of the old dog. Even if he did catch her and nip her, her tough rear end wouldn't feel a thing.

Martha would then look for Terrible Tom the turkey. He was quite a quiet boy before he met Martha, but she discovered a great way of teasing him. If she pulled his tail feathers he would get really cross. The more she pulled the nastier he got. Finally he would puff up all his feathers and start gobbling at her as loud as he could. He would flap his wings and try to chase her away, but she would only oink at him and try to pull out more feathers. Eventually Tom had enough and would jump on the tractor to escape.

As Martha made her way around the barnyard she would look for her favorite friend Harriet the Heifer. They were the same size. The two of them would run down the brook to cool off. They would roam the fields eating grass and looking for apples. They just loved being together. Martha often thought she was a cow rather than a pig. For that matter she often thought she was a person rather than a pig.

CHAPTER 6

THE BULL

One hot summer day Tony the Bull was feeling quite grumpy. He hated the hot weather and the other cows irritated him. But what irritated him the most was Martha and Harriet having fun while he felt so grumpy. Tony wanted Martha to go away. He would stomp around huffing and puffing and threatening to charge. All the other cows would watch and even Willy, the baby steer, would watch in amazement and admiration. He wondered how long it would be until his father would charge and knock Martha down. In anticipation all the cows began to give Tony some space. They knew how angry he could get. Martha couldn't have cared less about him and continued to play with Harriet. Suddenly Tony lunged towards Martha but she quickly stepped aside. Now she realized Tony was serious.

Tony, weighing at least 2,000 pounds, ran at Martha again. Just as he was about to smash into her and break all her ribs, Martha twisted round, reached up and grabbed Tony by the throat. She hung onto the loose flap of skin just under his neck for dear life. Poor Tony was so startled that he started to panic. Never in all his life had any creature dared to fight back. In his panic he started running in circles and bucking up and down. It was not only hard for a 2,000-pound bull to run around with a 700-pound pig around his neck, but it was embarrassing. Eventually poor Tony ran out of steam and came to a halt. It was only then that Martha let go of her grip on his throat. From that day on Tony never considered bothering Martha again; it would have been too humiliating.

CHAPTER 7

THE PARTY

Aunt Kate decided to throw a big party. It was to be a very special occasion. All kinds of people were going to come from far and wide. Aunt Kate decided to make it a splendid event. She rented a big tent and set up tables and chairs. The tables were set up with beautiful white tablecloths, silverware, napkins and candles. Aunt Kate arranged for a wooden dance floor to be put down on the lawn and for a band to play. She hired a caterer to provide the most delicious foods. This was to be a truly great party.

But all this strange activity unsettled the barnyard animals. They weren't getting all the attention they were used to and no one liked it. To make matters worse Aunt Kate had missed one of Martha's shrimp dinners. This was bad enough but she was confined for the day to her newly mended pen. She was not happy.

The day of the party dawned and it was a glorious day. The tables were covered with colorful flowers from the garden and everything was just perfect. Martha peeped through the slats in her pen and saw all the guests arriving. She was annoyed at not being invited to the party, after all this was her farm. The final insult as far as Martha was concerned was seeing all that lovely food on the table. She felt very sorry for herself but gradually this turned to anger.

The more she saw the madder she got until she decided to do something about it. She jumped up and threw herself as hard as she could against the side of her newly mended pen. The impact of her weight splintered the pen wall and it crashed to the ground like a bundle of firewood. At the sound of splintering wood everyone looked up. One guest screamed, "Lookout! What's that heading towards us? It's as big as a cow but looks like a pig."

Martha was really enjoying herself now and ran faster and faster towards the party. The first table that Martha hit flew up in the air and over on its side spilling food and drink everywhere. Guests were screaming and running around trying to escape this rampaging pig. But Martha just kept moving. It was so easy to go under the table and tip it over. This was exciting. Suddenly there was all this most scrumptious food all over the ground and Martha was eating it as fast as she could. She even grabbed food from a man's hand as she ran past him.

The party was a disaster. Unchecked Martha would overturn all the tables. In despair Aunt Kate had to think fast. She dashed to the remaining upright table and grabbed a giant platter of shrimp and cocktail sauce. Martha's favorite.

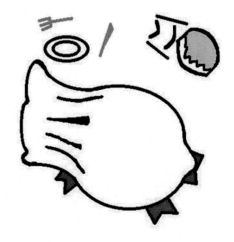

Waving this magnificent banquet of shrimps in front of Martha stopped her dead in her tracks. Aunt Kate spoke quietly and softly to her and led her into the old stables at the back of the farmhouse where she was locked up for the rest of the party.

But Martha loved these clean cool stables. She had a bowl of fresh water and the biggest platter of shrimps she had ever laid eyes on. She couldn't go dancing but she was happier than she ever thought possible.

From that day forward Martha's new home was the old stable. It was cool in the summer and warm in the winter. Here there were no flies to bother her and she was content, and so was everyone else.

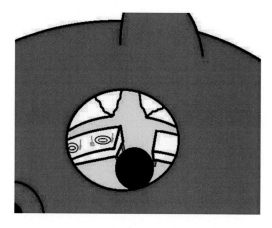

Printed in the United States
By Bookmasters